OUR AMERICAN DREAM

OUR
AMERICAN
DREAM

Cultivating a Life of
Success, Joy, and *Purpose*

ANDREW SAMUEL

LIONCREST
PUBLISHING

OUR AMERICAN DREAM
Cultivating a Life of Success, Joy, and Purpose

ISBN 978-1-5445-0218-2 *Paperback*
        978-1-5445-0219-9 *Ebook*

To Jane. This book was inspired by you. For thirty-nine years we have been together as college friends, husband and wife, parents, and grandparents. I love you deeply, and I am so grateful for all your support, encouragement, and love. Thank you.

I would also like to thank all of the people I have worked with over the years. Thank you for the opportunity to lead you and to be led by you. You have given me the opportunity to live out my dream of impacting people's lives positively!

Contents

___

Introduction

———

How does a poor, skinny little kid from India go from poverty to ringing the opening bell at Nasdaq? How does an average student go from mediocrity to building successful regional banks, taking three companies public, and buying and selling banks for millions of dollars? I don't ask this as a rhetorical question—I ask this as the formerly poor, skinny kid and average student. As someone who was able to rise out of poverty, I have some advice that I believe will help you become successful, but before I can share it with you, I have to tell you my story.

My life began in India, where I lived in a fourteen-by-fourteen-foot room with a cow dung floor. I lived with my parents, siblings, six of my aunts and uncles, and my grandparents. It was no secret to us that we lived in poverty. We had no indoor plumbing or electricity—if my siblings and I wanted to do our homework after dark, we had to go outside and sit underneath street lamps to complete it. We barely had enough to eat. My mother often encouraged us to sleep on our stomachs so we wouldn't be kept awake by the hunger pangs.

My father was a military man, so he traveled most of the time and was rarely home. He worked hard to earn three hundred dollars per year, and fifty of it went to my grandmother, who was blind and bedridden. I can only describe our life as a constant struggle—we shed countless tears, and we did all that we could to scrape by.

COW DUNG AND THE SPIRIT OF ENTREPRENEURSHIP

The average American probably knows a few facts about India. For instance, they know that it's a large country and that cows are sacred and honored. They wander freely about the land, and no one bothers them. However, few may know that cow dung is extremely useful. It makes an excellent sealant and burns well as fuel when it's dry. We often smeared it onto our dirt floors to seal in dust, making creative patterns before it dried. We also made cow dung patties and used those in lieu of wood for cooking over open fires. This may sound disgusting, but honestly, the cow dung didn't smell bad!

My family was always in need of additional income, and

we knew the value of cow dung, so we followed cows around and waited until they did their business. Then we collected their dung, formed cow dung patties, and sold them to people in our community. We also collected and sold twigs and branches, as firewood was hard to come by in India—people were willing to pay for it. We collected and sold whatever we could find because we needed money to put food in our stomachs. Every able-bodied person in the family made an effort to bring in money; the children sought out ways to make money for the family.

My parents were married, but with my father away for eleven months out of the year, my mother was essentially a single mom. She raised the children on her own for many years. Her days were filled with numerous tasks and responsibilities. She did an excellent job of teaching and caring for us, but she didn't stop there. She was a skilled seamstress, and she brought in additional income by hand-stitching blouses for women to wear underneath their *saris*, a traditional Indian garment. Later, she taught my two older sisters to sew. We were resourceful because we needed to survive. Looking back, I can see that our family "businesses" were created in the spirit of entrepreneurship, and at a very young age that spirit came alive in me.

WHAT'S IN A NAME?

I assumed that our family would always live this way. Poverty was all that I knew, and I never dreamed of another kind of life. Little did I know my father was about to receive an opportunity that would positively change our circumstances.

In 1964, Zambia, the African country formerly known as Northern Rhodesia, won their independence from the British, and that event created an incredible opportunity for my father. To summarize my father's opportunity without getting into a long history lesson, Zambia did not want to align with the US or the Soviet Union; instead, they recruited skilled military professionals from India because we were a neutral country. My father was one recruit among thousands of hopefuls, and it appeared that his chances were slim. However, God demonstrated His mighty hand in the selection process.

As the Zambian officials looked through thousands of résumés and portfolios, they became frustrated with trying to pronounce long, traditional Indian names. They finally decided that it was too difficult, and they would hire applicants with names they could pronounce. They hired eighty men with Christian names like Paul, Joseph, Thomas, and *Samuel*. It was amazing how God used my father's name to give him a new opportunity, but I had to remember that my father had a role in this coming to pass as well. None of this would have happened if he hadn't taken the initiative to apply.

This job was our ticket out of poverty, but it also meant that our family had to move from India to Zambia. We had to leave our extended family and our culture behind to start a new life on a completely different continent. This was the move of a lifetime. We knew it was going to be difficult, but my father chose this for us because it would improve our quality of life. His willingness to do whatever was necessary for the family led to educational and cultural opportunities that never would have been possible for me had we remained in India.

TEN YEARS IN ZAMBIA

I spent the next ten years attending primary, middle, and high school in the diverse country of Zambia. We lived alongside people of African, Indian, European, and Chinese origin, with most of them being skilled doctors, engineers, accountants, and teachers. It was a blessing to be in that global environment because we learned about different cultures by living with them, and it helped us learn how to embrace all people. We also learned how to communicate effectively through cultural differences.

In addition to learning and growing in diversity, my parents continually talked about the incredible educational opportunities that we had before us. They drilled into us that school was our training ground for college—since our family wouldn't have the money to send us to college, we needed to earn the grades to get scholarships.

THE AMERICAN DREAM FORMULA

Through hard work, God's favor, and a little bit of luck, I was eventually able to attend an American college in Pennsylvania. At this point, academic achievement was a higher priority than it had ever been, but no matter how hard I tried, my grades were always average at best. I couldn't cross the threshold to become an outstanding student. I'm sharing this with you because I didn't achieve success through academics—I gradually became successful by adhering to certain values that I learned throughout my life. Together, these values create what I call "The American Dream Formula." I'll discuss each of these values in detail throughout the book, along with how you can apply them in your personal and professional life to achieve success, but for now, here's a preview.

FOCUS

With social media and technology creating all of the distractions we face today, I believe the value of *focus* is slipping from our grasp. Focus is a value that I couldn't help but learn in my life, because in India, our family had to focus on survival; we had to earn money to buy food for our bellies. In Zambia, our focus was on education.

If we became distracted, we'd miss out on opportunities to create a better life for ourselves. It was difficult living in poverty at the beginning of my life, yet the desire to escape it cultivated the value of focus, which still continues to serve me well to this day.

PERSISTENCE

My parents demonstrated the value of persistence to us from an early age. They had a tremendously strong work ethic and a will to get us as far away from poverty as possible. They never gave up on their hopes and dreams for our family, and what they taught me worked to my advantage while I attended school in Zambia. I followed my parents' example and worked hard. I was absolutely committed to improving the quality of my life and that of the rest of our family, and I knew I could do that by getting good grades and getting into an American college. This persistent attitude still drives me today. I don't give up easily—when I have my mind set to accomplish something, I won't stop until I get it done.

FAITH

Focus and persistence are essential values, but they will only get you so far. They cannot work without faith, which is the most important part of the formula. I believe that God favored me with opportunities because my purposes were pure and right. He could see my heart and my commitment to serving and positively impacting people, and he led me on the path to success—to my American Dream—because I wanted to do more than just make money or build a name for myself. My motivations were not egocentric. I wanted to create a lasting, positive impact on people, and I was only able to do so with God's favor.

YOUR AMERICAN DREAM

The title of this book is *Our American Dream* because everyone's dream is unique. My dream may look very different from yours, and yours may look different from that of other people. No matter what it is, I believe that you have the ability to achieve it, as long as you keep your eyes open and apply the principles of the American Dream Formula. This country is unique in that you don't need to be born into privilege, have a high IQ, or another special advantage to be successful. The opportunities are endless, and everyone has the potential to do something amazing with their life!

The American Dream is alive and well, and it can be yours if you choose to pursue it. Even if you were born into favorable circumstances and the world is being offered to you on a platter, you can still apply these values to your life and increase your level of success. As you read this book, I want you to think about what you truly want for your life and begin working toward it. It doesn't matter if your goals are personal or professional; you can apply the values of the American Dream Formula, and they will work for you. Integrating focus, persistence, faith, and other key principles into my life have helped me to achieve my goals, and I believe they will help you achieve yours. I invite you to turn the page, continue reading about the American Dream Formula, and learn how you can begin to apply it in your life.

PART ONE

THE AMERICAN DREAM FORMULA

CHAPTER ONE

Focus

———

When I was young, I learned the critical value of focus through necessity; there weren't any distractions while living with fifteen other people in a single room with a cow dung floor. We didn't have the distractions of TV, sports, or hobbies—we lived simple lives from day to day and worked to put food on the table. Our singular focus was on where our next meal would come from, and nothing else mattered.

When I was older and we were able to eat regular meals, our focus shifted to education—we were driven by the promise that it was the way out of poverty. We never thought about playing soccer or football, taking dance lessons, or participating in any extracurricular or leisure activities. Our path was clear: get good grades, go to college, and improve our quality of life.

LET'S GET PRACTICAL

The ability to focus sounds simple enough: dedicate attention and energy to a particular task and tune out the noise and distractions. Focus is arguably one of life's most important skills, but with the constant demands on our time and the fast pace of our lives today, it can be challenging to maintain—we are easily distracted and find numerous ways to veer off track.

As a family man and CEO, I'm inundated with various tasks every day, but I manage to get them done. My sons-in-law have asked me how I'm able to accomplish so much in one day, and I say, "Hey, guys. It's all about being intentional. You have to train yourself to see that if you don't cross every item off your to-do list, your day is unfinished. You have to create a plan, follow through with it, and be disciplined enough to stay the course. You can't let peripheral things distract you from your path. Don't procrastinate, and set time limits for excess or unnecessary activity."

I realize that today, more than ever, distractions can easily interfere with our focus, but we must be determined to push past them. In the sections that follow, I'll address these obstacles and introduce habits I have put into practice in an effort to follow my own advice: the Sunday Night List, Online Time Limits, and Phone Control.

OBSTACLE ONE: PROCRASTINATION

Our human nature wants to leave undesirable tasks for last (or leave them behind altogether), but oftentimes, doing those tasks first will yield the highest benefits and impact. For example, I don't particularly like making sales calls, and I used to put them off, but now I make it a priority to do them first thing each day. I'd much rather call my friend to talk about the basketball game we're attending, but I don't allow myself to do so until I've called five prospects. That way, I get those calls off my mind, get paid, and I'm free to focus on the upcoming basketball game.

The same goes for when I need to have a disciplinary discussion with an employee regarding poor performance. These meetings are never pleasant and usually involve cutting their salary to some extent—can you blame me for wanting to put these off? However, by having these meetings right away, I'm able to help and coach the employee sooner rather than later, and I'm free to focus on more pleasant tasks without the dreaded meeting looming over me.

THE SUNDAY NIGHT LIST

Besides sheer willpower, is there a practical way to conquer procrastination? I've found that there is. Every Sunday night, I take time to look at what the upcoming week has in store, determine my top-priority tasks, and make a list. First, I write down of all of the tasks I *don't* want to do, but have to, and devise a plan to get them done early in the week. This sets me up for success and allows me to enjoy the latter part of my week as well as the weekend.

OBSTACLE TWO: THE INTERNET

I'm a big sports fan, and I enjoy going online to check scores and look at highlights. However, if I let myself get carried away, three hours can disappear in a heartbeat, and I know I'm not the only one facing this issue. I often see younger people in their twenties and thirties in airports, restaurants, and stores engrossed in the online world of sports, social media, or YouTube videos. Before you know it, they've spent half of their waking hours being unproductive, and they've done nothing to improve the direction of their life or their vocation.

Unfortunately, what was originally designed to be innovative and convenient is diluting our ability to focus. Many young professionals spend too much time on social media, and it's killing their motivation. It also hinders them from having meaningful relationships because they can't relate to others; it seems they only know how to communicate online and lack the ability to speak to people face-to-face.

And young professionals aren't the only ones being affected—children are being robbed of their parents' time and attention because they too are caught up in social media. For this reason, those parents aren't able to focus on nurturing their kids, and some even allow their children to play video games for hours on end. The result has been the development of suboptimal attention spans, with children knowing nothing about the art of writing or the joy of reading. It's quite sad.

ONLINE TIME LIMITS

I realize that I've painted a negative picture of the online world, but it doesn't have to be that way. Spending time on social media and other sites can be positive and serve to enhance your life when you are willing to make changes and do it right. Start by asking yourself if you are spending too much time online. If you find that you are, I challenge you to be more disciplined with the time that you spend "connecting" with others.

A good starting point for change is to assess your connection methods. Do you truly need to be on multiple platforms and sites, chatting with people in different ways, or can you choose one platform that is best suited for you and stick with it? Even then, it's important to set limits on the time you spend scrolling through that site. I suggest a thirty-minute limit at a designated time of day so it doesn't eat into your productivity. And there's an added bonus to doing this: setting limits will make the time you do spend online much more purposeful.

TRUE CONNECTION

The purpose of social media is to foster connection, but the truth is that it can be very isolating. I urge you to do all you can to prevent it from isolating you. Make it a point to interact with people face-to-face every day. Every career requires a certain level of ability to build relationships with peers, vendors, and leaders, and these relationships cannot be built on social media. They must be built in person using your eyes, voice, facial expressions, and body language. Failure to do so will result in your relationships diminishing in quality, and that won't get you any closer to your American Dream.

OBSTACLE THREE: CELL PHONES

Cell phones are convenient, but they can also be a terrible impediment to our focus. The minute we receive a call, email, or text, we drop everything to answer or send a response. This pattern quickly consumes the focus that we have on our tasks, so we must be careful and intentional about the time we spend on our phones—we can't allow it to dictate our schedules or the flow of our days.

PHONE CONTROL

To minimize the chances of being distracted by my phone, I schedule a few times during the day to check and respond to messages. I've found this to be an effective way to avoid being tied to the unpredictability of incoming messages and calls—and when I do respond, I'm able to fully focus on each message.

There's another habit I practice to help me strike a balance with my phone *and* get a good night's sleep at the same time: I turn off my phone at night. I don't leave it on silent—*I actually shut it down*. Leaving the phone on silent still keeps you tuned in to the vibration, and you may not feel settled because you have one eye closed and the other one on the phone. Now, you might be thinking, "Turn my phone *off*? What if someone calls or texts? What if there's an emergency?" While it's true that someone may need to reach you in the middle of the night, the likelihood is very low; people don't need to have access to you 24/7. And if you have a home phone, then that problem is solved.

I also look for opportunities to intentionally be without my phone. For example, when I go for walks, I leave my phone at home. I believe that having the phone on me during that time is a burden, and it takes away from the unwinding and cleansing experience of the walk. I'd much rather enjoy nature and focus on genuine interaction with my neighbors.

NATURAL TALENTS AND STRENGTHS

Another effective and straightforward way to improve your focus is to tap into your distinct skillset. But *how* do you discover that skillset? How do you know that you will excel in a certain field or in a certain area of expertise?

In the business world, powerful tests and tools are available, such as Myers-Briggs and StrengthsFinder to discover individual characteristics, strengths, and weaknesses, and they are often quite accurate. In fact, every company that I've worked with has used some type of assessment to determine the best roles for employees within their organization, but testing is just one of many ways to find your strengths.

A more innate approach to identifying your strengths is to have an open ear to those around you. Family, peers, and people in your community can give you their honest opinions and feedback. You can take into account what they say and act upon it, but you must be realistic.

To give you an example of what I mean, many people in my industry announce that they want to be a leader, and immediately, they are gung-ho to develop a plan. Their enthusiasm is wonderful, but I am candid with them and explain that while it is excellent to aspire to become a leader, they first need to understand the difference between managing and leading.

When you *manage,* you direct people to complete a specific set of tasks; when you *lead,* you employ a vision and strategy, and inspire others to achieve higher levels of performance. If a particular individual is better suited to manage, I encourage them to accept and embrace that their talents lie in the management arena—that's where they will be most likely to succeed. Problems arise when a nonleader continues to seek leadership roles; they are unfulfilled because leadership does not fall within their natural strengths. When it comes to your career, it's important to recognize your natural strengths and focus accordingly.

I don't just give the above advice to my employees; my family members see me as a leader, and they want to jump on the bandwagon. They say that they want to be inspirational company leaders or CEOs, and I never hesitate to tell them the truth: they need to think about what will make them happy for the next thirty or forty years. If that means being a high performer who doesn't manage or lead others, that's perfectly okay. If you aren't naturally talented in coaching or confrontation, forcing yourself into that arena will be uncomfortable for you and for your staff. There's great value in being a solid, productive employee, especially when you're fulfilled in what you do!

THE STARBUCKS EXPERIENCE

Starbucks, the popular American coffeehouse chain, is a

great example of the success of focus in action, but they also illustrate what can happen when you lose sight of your natural strengths. The company began selling coffee, a drink that has been around for hundreds of years, but when they made the decision to focus on the coffee *experience*, they became wildly successful—they made experience the foundation of their business model and allowed no outside distractions.

However, in recent years, Starbucks began deviating from this model. They introduced breakfast items and other products, and this created some challenges for the company. The baristas who once considered making coffee drinks an art form became distracted because they had to heat up egg sandwiches in addition to making drinks. They didn't have the time to take pride in their creations as they once did. Once they had to think about selling and preparing other products besides coffee, the quality of the drinks declined.

Starbucks realizes that drifting away from the initial focus that made them a household name has diluted their appeal, and they are now working to reboot their processes and strategy.* They're fully aware that to regain their position at the top of their coffee empire, they must

---

* Graham Robertson, "Case Study: Starbucks Come-Back Story: Lost Focus, Only to Regain It!" LinkedIn, April 20, 2015, https://www.linkedin.com/pulse/case-study-starbucks-come-back-story-lost-focus-only-regain-graham.

return to what made them great in the first place, and the same holds true for all of us. We will be most successful in this world when we focus on using our strengths and talents.

ADVERSITY AS A CATALYST OF FOCUS

While it's true that there are things we can do to better develop our ability to focus, adversity naturally pushes us to develop that skill throughout our lives. When we face tough decisions or formidable tasks, those challenges give us no choice but to focus on an end goal. I believe that I needed to face adversity in childhood to discover the value of focus and how to leverage it for success.

If you have never faced adversity, you can still develop focus and find success, but you may have to work much harder to do so. If you've had an easy, comfortable life, chances are you've never been in a situation that demanded your full focus to achieve success. A lack of challenges in life can hinder the development of focus, so if and when adversity comes your way, welcome it as an opportunity to cultivate strength and focus for the future. Simply put, adversity makes us tougher. It forces us to step back and say, "How do I remove distractions and stay focused on my goal? How can I keep my eyes on the things that will improve my outcomes?"

WISDOM THROUGH TRIAL AND ERROR

Adversity is an effective way to learn the value of focus, but we can also develop this skill through trial and error. And you don't necessarily have to be the one conducting the trials—you can learn through the example that others set and what they do and don't do.

For instance, I've been fortunate enough to gain wisdom from several motivating and influential leaders throughout my career. I worked with three dynamic CEOs in particular who helped me reflect upon who I am and what I do well.

The first CEO was an old-school banker who learned to lead and manage in the 1950s and 1960s. He had a dictatorial, command-and-control style, and he taught me the power of staying strong. The second leader was very analytical and good with numbers and ratios—he showed me the power of detail. The third leader invested in people, spent time with his employees, and showed empathy and care.

By working with these three leaders and observing their different leadership styles, I learned how to embrace my own natural style. I was able to step back and ask, "Which of these styles do I emulate? Which one comes naturally?" I discerned that the command-and-control style was not in my character; I wasn't one to demand results and elicit responses out of fear. I did have a love for numbers, but I only enjoyed them up to a certain point, and I didn't have that strong of a grasp on financials.

After thinking it through, I decided that the third leadership style was most natural for me. I believed that God had given me the ability to show empathy, and as time went on, it became more and more obvious that this was the style that would be most fulfilling for me and for my employees. Once I began to apply this leadership style to my professional life, I experienced success in various ventures.

FOCUS AND OUR AMERICAN DREAM

I had a difficult adjustment when I first moved to the United States to attend college. I transitioned into a new culture and had to begin learning within a new educational system. I encountered some challenges that I'll discuss in detail a bit later in the book, but in summary, I had a lot on my mind, which caused me to lose focus on my studies. As a result, my GPA during my freshman year of college was 1.67, and I graduated with a 2.2 cumulative GPA. These were far from admirable results, but focus helped me to overcome my gaps in knowledge or struggles with coursework. I studied longer and harder than other students did for exams, did extra project work, and had one-on-one meetings with professors to learn more about certain subjects. I carried that drive and work ethic into my professional career, and for the last thirty-five years, I have spent time building fast-growing, values-based banks that have experienced tremendous success. I recognize that I'm not a brilliant person, but my laser focus and will to accomplish things have allowed me to be triumphant in life.

The best advice I can give when it comes to focus is not to worry about what anyone else wants you to be. Once you discover your strengths and talents and hone them, you will live a very fulfilling life. No matter your age, level of education, background, or career status, it's never too late to focus on your strengths, develop them, and get closer to your American Dream.

CHAPTER TWO

Persistence

———

In Chapter One, we established that focus is a critically important value in becoming successful. However, it can't stand alone. It is nothing without *persistence*—the sustained, long-term attention to an area of focus.

I learned the value of persistence from my mother, who modeled it very well. She never completed high school, and in an Indian society that already deemed women as second-class citizens, her lack of education made life even more difficult. In spite of (or perhaps because of) her own experience, she knew that her children needed an education to escape the grip of poverty, and she worked tirelessly to make that happen for us.

She had little education, but she was a skilled seamstress and spent countless hours stitching blouses for Indian saris. At first, she only finished and sold one blouse a day, as she did this work with her bare hands. But she persisted, and eventually she saved enough money to buy a sewing machine. With the sewing machine and the help of my sisters, she was able to increase her output to five or six blouses per day.

Persistence was the obvious driving force for my mother through all of her efforts. She had her heart and mind set on a goal for her children, and she did all that she could to make that goal a reality—she never gave up. I admired the way she pushed herself in her work, and I'm truly thankful for her example. The lessons I learned from watching her in my early years played a big role in the development of my strong persistence.

IT REALLY DOES PAY OFF

Back in 1984, the United States was in the midst of a recession, and job opportunities for college graduates were scarce. I had been working the night shift at a local restaurant so I could look for a job during the day. I called businesses to try and land interviews, but I was told no over and over again; I began to think I would never make any progress toward my goals. Despite this concern, I stubbornly persisted and continued to make phone calls—I had to find a good job so I could support my family.

After a while, I figured out that making phone calls

between 8:00 and 5:00 on workdays was futile; I wasn't able to get past receptionists and other gatekeepers to talk with a decision maker. I changed my strategy and began calling after 6 p.m., when leaders might be working late at the office. I called a local bank after 6:00, and the vice president of Personnel answered. He told me that there weren't any openings, but I told him that I believed I could make a difference in the organization and asked for fifteen minutes of his time. After a bit of convincing, he agreed to interview me. My new strategy had worked!

When I arrived for the interview, the VP told me that his secretary recognized my name on the appointment list. She remembered me because I had left seventeen messages prior to reaching him directly. If that isn't a demonstration of persistence, then I'm not sure what is!

The interview went well, and the VP said that he saw something special in me. He hired me as a management trainee on the spot. Had I not been so persistent, I might not be where I am today, buying, growing, merging, and selling banks.

CHOCOLATE FOR EVERYONE

The story of Milton Hershey, the creator of Hershey's Chocolate, is an incredible, famous example of persistence. His classic chocolate is a global brand that is enjoyed throughout the world today. Most of us have enjoyed this delicious chocolate at one time or another, which makes it hard to believe that it almost never existed!

As crazy as this sounds, in the late nineteenth and early twentieth centuries, chocolate was a delicacy that was reserved for only the ultrawealthy—for people like the Rockefellers, Vanderbilts, and others of similar stature. The average consumer couldn't afford chocolate, but Milton Hershey believed that it could be mass produced for everyone to enjoy. He had a fourth-grade education and wasn't an engineer or experienced chocolatier, so before the Hershey Company became a reality, he had to file for bankruptcy *four times*. He could have easily given up after the first, second, or third bankruptcy, but he kept going. Had he not been so persistent, we wouldn't enjoy his delicious, world-famous chocolate today!

CLOSING THE GAP BETWEEN PROMISE AND DELIVERY

My persistence has been a great strength in all of my career. My reputation in banking has been built on my commitment to accomplishments—when I commit to something, I persist until it's done. This trait has been contagious within the banks I have worked with, and our employees know that when we set targets, we are expected to persist until we achieve them.

Through persistence, I've established myself as a man of my word, and people trust me. Every board of directors I've worked with knows that when I provide a strategic business plan with goals, we will achieve them. Since I've done this numerous times, our employees, customers, investors, and other constituents have come to expect consistent delivery from me.

PERSISTENCE IN THE BUSINESS WORLD

To provide a specific example of how persistence has paid off for me in business, several years ago, I had ninety days to open a new bank branch. We planned to open it in a historic building, so the state government and historical society had to sign off on the project before we could begin construction. The application process included a thirty-day waiting period, with no guarantee that it would be approved.

Rather than mailing the application and waiting around, our extremely persistent team walked to the state capital and delivered it in person. We explained what we were doing and why it was important for us to receive an answer as soon as possible—we hoped that we could convince their staff to act on it right away. As a result, we left the building with a signed authorization to proceed with construction the next day!

To give another example, we had to meet with the Federal Reserve, the state's Department of Banking, and FDIC before we could open our most recent bank. Our regulators informed us that it would be an eighteen- to twenty-four-month process, meaning we'd miss out on two years of opportunities. That time frame was too long for us, so we began to explore alternatives.

We found out that if we acquired a small, existing bank rather than creating a startup, we'd only have to wait six to eight months. This was better suited to our goals but still too long of a wait. So we persisted and continued to ask the regulators if we could open the bank sooner. After a lot of hard work and meticulous organization, we received approval for the bank within one hundred days!

I hope these examples have shown that you don't have to settle for less or for the status quo. You don't have to accept statements like, "That's the way it's always been." Tap into your persistent nature, push to achieve your goals, and make things happen!

PERSIST IN THE LITTLE THINGS

It's easy for us to find the motivation to persist in achieving big goals, but we need to have the same level of commitment when it comes to the little things.

Let's say you see an old friend at the grocery store, and

you make small talk about the weather and family. On this particular occasion, you ask, "How is everything going?" and they tell you that their son is recovering from surgery. You respond by saying that you will pray for them. But will you? If you say that you are going to pray for someone, make sure that you actually do it! Don't just say that you will because it's polite and you hope the words will make your friend feel better.

What does the above scenario have to do with persistence? *Everything.* Persistence starts with the little things, such as being forthright in everything you say. For example, people will say, "I'll call you tomorrow," and then they don't follow through. Phrases like, "I'll text you later," or "Let's have lunch next week," are often uttered, but the intent is not followed by action. Our society is almost to the point where we take what people say with a grain of salt, and there's no expectation for them to follow through.

To improve on this social epidemic and instill the value of persistence, I encourage you to start being sincere in the little things: don't speak, text, or email anything that you don't mean. If you say you're going to call someone tomorrow, then do it. If you promise to have a report done by Friday, do whatever it takes to get it done. If you tell your spouse that you will be home for dinner at 5:30, don't wander in at 5:45 or 6:00. Your words can't be vague, insincere statements—they are promises that must be followed by delivery. Practicing these behaviors will make you a more persistent, successful, and trustworthy individual.

DON'T GIVE UP ON PERSISTENCE

It takes discipline and training, but you *can* become a persistent person. Plan to take everything that you do to the finish line, and you will feel great pride and satisfaction in your work. You'll also build a winning reputation, which will lead to countless opportunities.

You don't need to be a rocket scientist or have a degree from Harvard to incorporate persistence into your life. Start by being sincere in your written and verbal statements. Stick with your commitments and live by your word.

I believe that the quality and fulfillment of your life will improve when you deliver on your promises and pursue that delivery with passion. If my family members and I were able to harness the power of persistence to create a cow dung business when I was a kid, I have no doubt that you can conquer the tasks in front of you. If you practice persistence a little bit at a time, eventually, you will rise above your challenges!

CHAPTER THREE

Faith

——

Faith has played a prominent role in my family for many generations and is still very important to us today. I strongly believe that the reason I went from being a skinny, hungry, poor kid in India to finding opportunities in America is because God answered my family's prayers.

When I was growing up, my mother prayed every day. She prayed on her knees with her arms wide open, prayed while sitting at the table, and prayed while standing up. She prayed silently, and she prayed out loud, her cheeks often wet with tears. She openly demonstrated that her faith was strong and that she fully trusted in God. She believed that He would provide opportunities for us to escape poverty and break free from our adversities, and she never wavered in her belief.

My mother's devotion goes back through our family lineage to a generation of Hindu priests in southern India. Long ago, one of my earliest forefathers encountered Anglican missionaries from England who introduced him to Christianity, and since then, our family has recognized and practiced the faith. We've incorporated it into our names as well: my last name, Samuel, was one of my ancestor's favorite prophets, and my first name, Andrew, was my grandmother's favorite disciple.

GRANDMOTHER'S FAITHFULNESS

My mother wasn't the only one in our family who had strong faith—my grandmother did as well. Due to cooking over open fires in confined spaces for more than thirty years, she went blind at the age of fifty-five. This resulted in her becoming housebound, and with nothing else to do, she sat on a mat and prayed all day long. She prayed for our daily meals and for our current needs to be met, but she also was proactive and prayed for future generations. She could have spent the time feeling sorry for herself, but she tirelessly prayed for others instead. Her faith, along with my mother's, had a profound impact on me as a child, and I still carry their example with me in my personal and professional life today.

I truly believe that God favors those who have pure and honest purposes, which is why He was faithful in answering the prayers of my mother and grandmother, and why I am always confident that He will honor my family's prayers.

NELSON MANDELA'S EXAMPLE

My faith has deep roots in my family, but I have also been greatly inspired by the faith of Nelson Mandela, the former president of South Africa.

After being convicted of sabotage and conspiring to overthrow the South African government, Nelson Mandela was imprisoned on Robben Island with nothing but time, and he spent much of it in prayer. He also worked on growing and developing his God-given skills. During his twenty-seven years in prison, he earned his bachelor's degree in law from the University of London, was a great mentor and encourager to fellow inmates, and wrote many political statements that were smuggled out of prison and shared with the oppressed people of South Africa.

After his release, he didn't plunge back into life and try to make up for everything he missed; he believed in a purpose that stretched beyond himself, and it was honest and pure. He flawlessly transitioned from prisoner to messenger of peace, and his steadfast commitment drove a movement to help free South Africa from apartheid.

In interviews, Mandela said he'd always had an unwavering conviction that he'd be released. He prayed for the grace and wisdom to make a difference. His strong faith helped him to survive twenty-seven years in prison and to unify South Africa into a peaceful nation. Mandela's work is an excellent example of three important aspects of faith that I encourage you to remember:

1. **Don't just pray for the present.** We can trust that God will answer prayers that are lifted up in genuine faith. However, we can't just pray for the present; we must pray for tomorrow, and for future generations as well.
2. **Apply your talents.** While prayer is important, you can't just pray and wait for something to happen—you have to apply your talents.
3. **Authentic action.** Don't do anything for selfish reasons; move forward with a true purpose that will benefit others.

The combination of prayer, applying your talents, and authenticity in action will allow your dreams to come to fruition.

DOORS WILL OPEN

By embracing and practicing the three aspects of faith, I believe that God will open doors for you at just the right time, and when He does, it will be a tremendously wonderful gift. I know that He's opened doors for me that otherwise would have been closed, had it not been for my faith!

My faith has been rewarded many times in my life. When I finished high school, I wanted to come to the US as an international student. There were many challenges, but somehow, circumstances lined up in my favor.

I wanted to attend Messiah College, a Christian, liberal arts school in Pennsylvania, and at the time, tuition cost $4,000 per year. My father only made $3,000 a year, so I had to conquer this financial challenge right away. The college staff was kind enough to encourage me to pursue work study with international aid and summer job opportunities so that I could afford my tuition.

International students also need an American family to sponsor them, and I had no contacts in the US. However, an American family found out about me through a mutual friend from Zambia, and they kindly offered to sponsor me! Through the power of faith and prayer, God opened doors for my education. In His goodness, He pulled me from adversity, and I truly believe He brought me here to fulfill His purposes in the banking community.

FAITH AND PURPOSE

I understand that we all have different circumstances in life, which means that some people may view situations from a mindset of faith while others may not. If you've never experienced trying circumstances, you may not have a compelling reason to develop a life of faith, but this doesn't mean that you never will, nor does it mean that you can't approach your life and career with purpose. What you choose to do cannot be rooted in greed, prestige, or your ego—it has to be about positively impacting the lives of others. You must look to your beliefs and inner strengths to build something bigger and greater than yourself.

I had this all wrong when I first began my career. I desperately wanted to be the vice president of a bank, and my mother asked me, "Well, what is your motivation behind that?" I told her that if I became a VP, I'd have a high salary, excellent benefits and perks, and people would take me seriously—it would mean that I had "arrived." She told me that it would never work out for me if those were the reasons why I wanted the job, which left me confused. What other reasons could there be?

She went on to ask me if the title would put me in a position to help and impact others positively, and then I understood what she meant. I had all the wrong motivations for wanting to become a VP. I figured out that I had been praying for the right thing but with the wrong motivations; I couldn't expect God to honor my request when my motivations were completely selfish.

After learning this important lesson, I go into every business venture with the intent of doing good and giving back to the community—I work to leave a positive impact in people's lives. I leverage my unique, God-given skills and talents to build companies that contribute to the community and make the world a better place. I believe that God will continue to bless my endeavors as long as my heart and purposes remain pure.

FAITH AND THE AMERICAN DREAM

By leaning on my faith, trusting in God's leadership, and applying my gifts with intention, I've gained the confidence to face challenges head-on. My past has given me a powerful faith. Nothing in my life or my career today can be as bad as what I experienced in my daily life as a child, and that keeps every obstacle in perspective. I believe that I can accomplish all that I set out to do, and I encourage you to believe the same about yourself. Find your inner strength and move forward with faith and conviction.

BEYOND THE AMERICAN DREAM FORMULA

Focus + Persistence + Faith has been my American Dream

Formula for success for as long as I can remember, and after reading Part 1, I hope that you will consider making it yours as well. It may take some work to incorporate these values into your life, but once they are instilled in you, they put you on the fast track to fulfillment.

Now, I invite you to dive in to Part 2, where I expand upon the formula, share the principles that I consider to be the keys to enduring happiness and success, and show you how to apply them in your daily life.

PART TWO

PRINCIPLES FOR ENDURING SUCCESS

CHAPTER FOUR

Authenticity

———

I was born in India, and I lived there until I was seven years old. During that time, I was part of a tight-knit, extended family and community; we had no television or newspapers, and little contact with the outside world, but we didn't feel deprived. We only knew the people and places around us, and living in this manner created a genuine, enduring authenticity within our community.

When my father decided to relocate our family to Zambia for a better life, our simple, authentic lifestyle came to an end. When we arrived in Zambia, we discovered that we were like fish out of water. We had our first ever encounters with African natives, and we found ourselves struggling with our identities in this new place—we had to assimilate into strange surroundings, a new culture, a new school, and new people.

Our first few months at school in Zambia were a time of significant hardship—we didn't understand English very well, the teachers spoke too fast, and our clothing from India did not fit in. We were made fun of constantly. Fortunately, a British teacher took an interest in our family and helped us slowly assimilate into school.

The adjustment was tough, but our circumstances were better than they had ever been in India—our family was making more money, and we gradually improved the quality of our lives.

A CULTURE SHOCK FOR GOOD

Ten years later, I found myself on another plane. This time, I was headed westward to the United States. When I landed, I chatted excitedly with a customs officer about my new school and asked him to tell me everything he knew about it. I thought surely there were only twenty-five to thirty schools in the entire country. I was tremendously shocked when the officer informed me that there were thousands of colleges. I had no idea how big America really was, and I was in for a few more surprises.

When I arrived at the college campus, I saw people looking at food in large plastic cases, inserting money, and then retrieving the food. I learned that these contraptions were called "vending machines," and I thought they were incredible! Then, when I ate at the school cafeteria, I saw the other students using knives and forks to eat. This may seem like no big deal, but I had never used these tools before in my life. I didn't want to be the only one eating with my hands, so I watched and mimicked the other students until I learned how to properly use silverware.

It definitely took time for me to get acclimated to the food, people, surroundings, and culture; it felt very much like the adjustment period I went through when I first moved to Zambia, but this time it was a little bit easier. Growing up in a multicultural environment gave me an advantage: it enabled me to be true to myself. I could be authentic, and that helped me to relate to others easily. I also had the advantage of having experienced three different "lives," viewing the world through three different perspectives: Andrew from India, Andrew from Zambia, and now, Andrew in America.

I define authenticity as being real. It's simply being yourself and being true to who and what you are. Your choice of words, tone, and mannerisms are uniquely yours and display your personal brand of authenticity to others. I've also found that being candid and vulnerable is another big part of being authentic. Sharing these stories about my life and my struggles have helped me reveal my true self to others.

I'M NOT A BANKER

In the midst of moving around all the time, I discovered that the only constant in my life was *myself.* I had to stay comfortable and grounded in who I was. Living on three different continents and relocating numerous times have helped me to establish comfort and security in being authentic, particularly in the areas where I live and work.

For example, before anyone ever acknowledges me as a bank executive, they say, "Andrew is a great person, and he gets along with everyone. He's *real.*" To me, that is the ultimate compliment because even though I am a bank executive, I don't want to be identified as one. I want to be known as the kind, authentic leader that I strive to be; I don't want to be viewed as a pretentious leader with a big ego. Some leaders feel the need to wear expensive suits and drive eye-catching cars to feel secure in their roles and don't believe they have the freedom to be their true selves. Instead of considering how they can positively impact others, they get caught up in their image, their title, or selfish obsessions, and that's just not me.

THE REAL WARREN BUFFETT

American magnate and investor Warren Buffett is an ideal example of a humble leader who desires to be known for who he is, not for what he does. Despite his net worth, he is no frills and down to earth. When people ask him for his magic formula of investing, he doesn't throw out pretentious terms and fancy stock market acronyms. He simply says, "There's nothing to it. Just invest in good management teams and set clear financial goals." He treats everyone equally regardless of their status, and he is as well known for his investing skills as he is for being humble and authentic.

His humble mindset is also reflected in his choice of clothing, where he eats, and where he lives. His modest home in Nebraska and the old Buick in his driveway certainly don't announce his world-renowned stature and wealth. He is an average person who loves Cheetos and Coke, and as such, people can relate to him. He's an inspiration to many from different walks of life.

While his humility is refreshing, we can't forget his philanthropic nature that speaks volumes about his authenticity. He has given billions of dollars to his three children's foundations to support the various causes that his children are passionate about. And finally, he has made a commitment to give 99 percent of his assets to charity throughout his lifetime.* What a generous spirit!

THE FAMILY VAN

I drive my daughter's old minivan to work every day. She has young triplets and had a greater need for a new vehicle, so I bought one for her family instead of for myself. My staff laughs at me when I pull up in a five-year-old Toyota Sienna with high mileage and scratches on the side, but it doesn't bother me. They tell me that I should drive a luxury car, but I don't feel that would be practical. The world can chuckle if they want, but it won't change anything because my identity is strong. This is who I am, and most people appreciate my authentic nature. So I'll continue to lead the way in my minivan!

---

* "How Can Warren Buffet Be So Rich if He Has Donated 99% of His Money to Charity," Quora.com, https://www.quora.com/How-can-Warren-Buffett-be-so-rich-if-he-has-donated-99-of-his-money-to-charity.

STRENGTH IN VULNERABILITY

Authenticity enhances our lives because it draws people to us. If you are a business leader, this will be of great benefit to you because people will know that they are getting the "real deal" when they interact with you. However, if you want to be truly authentic, you can't just reveal your strengths; you'll have to reveal your weaknesses and vulnerabilities as well.

To give an example of how I share my vulnerabilities, most people assume that I had a 4.0 GPA all the way through college, but I didn't. I finished with a 2.2. While I'm not proud of my academic performance, I'm very open about it. I believe that sharing about my less-than-ideal track record allows others to be comfortable around me. In fact, my mediocre GPA often sparks inspirational conversations—people start to believe that they can accomplish great things, no matter their grades.

To give another example, I have five daughters, and every single one of them has experienced challenges and made poor choices here and there. I love them dearly, and I'm always there for them; they take priority over my business commitments. On more than one occasion, I've had to leave executive staff meetings due to concerns that I had at home. I've had to say, "Folks, I'm sorry, but I'm in no mental state to engage in today's meeting. I'm dealing with a personal issue and need to focus on that. Please excuse me, I'm going to step out for a bit."

I'm sure most leaders wouldn't do that, but if I'm able to fully engage with others, I feel the need to tell them. It's only fair to let them know that I can't give them my full attention at the moment. Being authentic and honest builds strong bonds with your teams, and they will follow you with dedicated loyalty.

BIG MOVES

I talk quite a bit about authenticity building loyalty because I've experienced it firsthand. At one point, I had to move and temporarily relocate the business to Florida, and some of my key staff moved right along with me. Some of them had to take pay cuts, but they moved anyway. Then, after a successful transition, most of them returned to Pennsylvania with me. They didn't follow me because I'm some sort of a pied piper or a genius; they joined me because I have always been real with them and they wanted to continue working with an authentic leader.

FREEDOM IN AUTHENTICITY

My people know me well, and they know that they don't have to do things my way; if I express displeasure with something, they don't have to change it. They know that I will be honest and share what I think, but I respect them, and they know that it does not always have to be my way. I feel that's an unnecessary burden in any business. Being myself gives my staff the freedom to be themselves—they feel empowered to apply their creativity, voice their opinions, and find ways to grow without unrealistic expectations or backlash from me.

For example, our company leaders recently convened to discuss how our corporate colors of turquoise, purple, and white appeared in some new office branches. A couple of locations had purple walls that I thought looked horrible. They asked me to share my thoughts on the color, and instead of using my position to get my way, I said, "I'm not a fan. I don't think it looks good, but if you guys like it, that's fine. It's not that big of a deal." Ultimately, they changed the color, but it was their decision, not mine.

AUTHENTIC LEADERSHIP

If you are a leader or manager of people, you not only face your own challenges, but you also encounter challenges with your employees. If you're dealing with someone who displays poor values and performance, you can't put off having a conversation with them. I realize that these conversations are generally unpleasant, so we may procrastinate and tell ourselves that we'll get to it later, but we have to address these issues as soon as possible.

When you set up a meeting with the employee, don't

create any false pretenses, and don't sugarcoat your words. I like to begin these meetings with a coaching session to discuss and work through the problem and then move on to more upbeat items. This ends the meeting on a positive note. Nobody enjoys dealing with sticky personnel issues, but you must be intentional with your actions and decisions, and correct and encourage the employee.

Leaders also have to treat everyone with respect. No matter a person's position or role, you should give them the attention they deserve; everyone needs to feel important. To give an example of how I did this recently, I was late for a phone call and found myself rushing into the office. I rushed through the door of our headquarters, only to discover that six people were waiting to talk to me. I walked past them quickly, but I didn't brush them off. I said, "Everyone, I'm sorry. I'm late for a phone call and need to get to my office, but I will be back in an hour."

Had I rushed in and ignored everyone, they would have felt insignificant, and some might have taken it personally. As the leader, I can't blitz by people without greeting them, or without explaining why I'm in a hurry. When you find yourself in a situation like this, remember, it only takes a moment to tell people what is going on and to assure them that they are important to you. I believe that authenticity is powerful, inspiring, and encouraging, and we shouldn't minimize its importance. It doesn't matter if you are a leader or not—a few words can make a world of difference!

CHAPTER FIVE

Family

———

My wife and I have been married for thirty-six years, have five wonderful daughters, four sons-in-law, and twelve grandchildren. We had our first daughter when I was a senior in college. We were excited when we found out that we were expecting and decided at that moment that Jane would stay home while I worked to provide for our family. We were absolutely committed to Jane being a stay-at-home mom, even though it meant that we would have to make many sacrifices.

I was confident that we had made the right decision, but before then, my prime motivation for finishing school had been to find a job and help support my extended family. Suddenly, that motivation had to change. All at once, I was a brand-new dad, the sole provider for my immediate family, and a secondary provider for my extended family on another continent!

I had worked just enough while I was in school to make some money, but to be honest, I focused more on my social life than I did on academics or finances. I realized that I had to change my habits and strive to perform at a higher level if I was going to provide for two families. Having a crying baby at home and struggling relatives in India definitely changed my priorities—I could no longer live my life as a laid-back college student.

FRIENDS VS. FAMILY

Friendships are wonderful, but they change, and they come and go. Family is the foundation of our lives, and they provide a stable, safe, loving environment for us. I wouldn't be where I am today if my family hadn't supported and encouraged me; they had helped me develop my sense of purpose, and I knew that I wanted to provide for them as much as I could.

I have sixty extended family members in India, Europe, and the United States. All of them continue to motivate me to succeed, and I am ever so grateful to be able to give back and provide for them, even if it's only in small ways.

EXPENSES IN INDIA

Financial assistance to my family in India helps to cover

three major life expenses: education, marriage, and home ownership.

The first expense, education, is nonnegotiable. A large part of India is mired in poverty, and the only way out of poverty is through a good education. It's a high priority for me to help pay for the education of my nieces and nephews so they in turn have a chance to provide for generations down the line.

Wedding ceremonies in India are quite elaborate, resulting in the second large expense, marriage. Similar to the custom in America, the bride's family covers the cost of the wedding, but there is much more to it. The bride's family gives the groom or the groom's family a *dowry*, or a transfer of wealth for the benefit of the bride. This can include money, gold, deeds to property, vehicles, or even a home, and I like to help the women in my family with this cost.

The third major expense in India is home ownership. Like everywhere else in the world, owning a home is one of life's biggest costs. Compared to average earnings, the cost of home ownership in India is extremely high, therefore, you need your extended family to help make it a reality. We have been fortunate to help some of our family in India and the United States achieve this dream of home ownership.

I know that every additional dollar I earn can be used to better the lives of my immediate and extended family in various ways, and I wire money to family members on a regular basis. While some might think this is burdensome, I enjoy it. I don't believe that I exist just to take care of myself, or only my wife and my children—I am here to take care of a large family.

IT FEELS GOOD TO SHARE

Sharing accomplishments with others gives those accomplishments more meaning. To me, happiness is far more than simply having money. Making money is rewarding, but *giving it away* is much more rewarding! I want to share my success with others and have a positive impact on their lives. And when I see that impact, it drives me to work even harder.

CELEBRATING TOGETHER

I'm always happy to receive a promotion, but it's never because of the money. Of course, I know that making more money helps me to better support my extended family, but I enjoy celebrating the achievement with them more than I do the increase in income. Sharing accomplishments with loved ones makes them more meaningful, and I appreciate celebrations so much that I've incorporated them into our company processes.

Anytime we promote someone or an employee does something extraordinary, we give them recognition, and we make every effort to include their family or spouse in the excitement. For example, we might make dinner reservations at a high-end restaurant, and unbeknownst to the employee, we ask their spouse to arrive first. When the employee arrives, it's like a surprise party for them, and it also gives us the opportunity to thank and acknowledge the spouse. After all, the employee probably couldn't be successful without spousal support.

Acknowledging employees in front of their loved ones lets them know that we truly appreciate them. It also fosters company loyalty, creates a positive work environment, keeps everyone motivated and engaged, and strengthens the bond between team members. We place great value on the contributions of our employees' families, and their presence always adds more meaning to the celebration.

We also thank and acknowledge spouses and families during the holidays. We send a gift to our employees' homes with a note that says, "Dear spouse/significant other/family, we're so thankful for the way that you support John throughout the year. We thank you for your loyalty and for being an essential part of our company."

WORK/FAMILY BLEND

Technology has made businesses more efficient, allowing automated tasks to be completed at a fast pace, and it seems that some companies expect the same from their human employees—they try to squeeze every last drop of blood from them. I strongly disagree with this approach. It doesn't take much effort to acknowledge your staff and their family, and meshing work with family also improves employee performance and boosts morale.

One way that we support the work/family blend is by allowing our employees to designate seven days a year as "family days." We want to give our people quality time with their families, so if an employee's son is in a school play or if they want to attend a family reunion, we give them time off so they won't miss out on these events. Then they can return to work refreshed and ready to be productive!

THE ROCKEFELLER EFFECT

Roughly thirty years after the Civil War and throughout both World Wars, we saw the emergence of families like the Rockefellers. These families worked hard and became wealthy by taking advantage of opportunities to improve their quality of life and by establishing strong extended family values.

The Rockefellers started with very meager beginnings. They became the wealthiest family in the United States under the leadership of John D. Rockefeller, who created Standard Oil Company. The wealth created through this company secured their family legacy and well-being for generations to come. But it didn't stop there! The Rockefellers didn't just share money with their own extended family—they shared with many others and went on to be one of the most philanthropic families of all time. Their imprint is still all over the world today, with the Christmas tree lighting ceremony at Rockefeller Center in New York being one of America's most well-known events.

Even though many of us can't relate to the Rockefellers, who amassed billions of dollars in wealth, we can relate to their family values, and their goal of creating a legacy. My parents didn't have a college education, but they worked hard so that *I* could have one. As a result, college was a viable option for my children, and it's now an option for my grandchildren as well. When you aim to establish a family legacy, it positively impacts the present and will compound in the future.

FAMILY AT WORK

I'm proud to say that I've had at least one family member involved in every bank I've worked with. I welcome them into the business, under one condition: when they are at work, they can't expect special treatment. They are not my daughter, nephew, or any other relation during that time; they are an employee, and so am I. They can't call me Dad or Uncle or ask for any favors. Once we get into the parking lot after work, I might give them a giant hug, but when we're in the office, it's all business. It's awkward to draw that line sometimes, but it does work well for us!

You may think that working with family is difficult, but I've found it to be a unique and enriching experience. I look to build companies that impact people's lives, and my kids see the positive results of my efforts to work toward that goal. It's only natural that some of them want to work for the companies that I lead.

I can't stress enough the importance of embracing family as the foundation of our lives. They drive us toward our American Dream, and when we have supportive people to share our accomplishments with, those dreams mean so much more.

CHAPTER SIX

Service

———

Through life experience, I've learned that serving others is an essential step on the path to achieving success. Great leaders have a strong servant mindset, and they invest in the people around them: they help others grow and don't focus purely on their own gains.

I learned the importance of service while I was in college. I couldn't afford tuition, but the school offered many work opportunities to make money. I signed up for any and every job: I cleaned toilets, mopped floors, and washed windows. At that point in my life, I was simply grateful to be in school, and I appreciated every task that offered pay.

After I graduated, I got my first real job as the night shift manager at a local restaurant chain. Most nights after the bars closed, we experienced a rush hour that brought in a large crowd that was usually drunk. I had to motivate the waitstaff, cooks, and busboys to serve these rowdy customers who often acted like imbeciles. They'd had too much to drink and threw up in the bathroom or even in their seats, but we continued to serve them with smiles on our faces.

The night shift was unpleasant at best. Nobody wanted to mop up vomit or the other messes from the late crowd, and I didn't blame them. Since I couldn't ask the staff to do something that I wasn't willing to do myself, I took the lead on these duties. It would have been easy for me to delegate these disgusting jobs, but I wanted to show everyone that we were a team. When I finally did ask someone to clean the bathroom, they agreed because they had seen me do it. We became a cohesive unit because I was willing to serve them before I asked them to serve me.

GRANDFATHER'S INFLUENCE

When I look back on my willingness to clean up horrible messes, I believe this part of my value system came from my grandfather. He always said that no matter the circumstances, we should always serve others and work and behave in ways to develop a strong, trustworthy reputation. He often talked about the work ethic of a local family-owned shoe repair company to drive his point home. He said, "Have you ever seen anyone in the family-owned shoe repair company sitting under a tree, doing nothing? No, you haven't. That's because their family has been repairing shoes for five generations, they continue to excel at their trade, and they do it to serve others. It doesn't matter if you repair shoes or if you're the CEO of a big corporation—you always serve others and do your best."

My grandfather also urged me to have respect for all people. I was not to think more or less of anyone because of their job title, but rather, to form my opinion of them based on the quality of their performance. I believe that his insightful wisdom and my night shift management experiences have carried me through my career, and I've blended the two to develop our company's servant leadership model. In this model, we manage from the bottom up, instead of from the top down.

THE SERVANT LEADERSHIP MODEL

Instead of the dictatorial-style leadership that was common in the 1960s and 1970s, our company manages in a way that guides and inspires people; we want them to achieve a higher level of performance and embrace new challenges. We know that if our teams blossom and grow, the company will grow right along with them.

We illustrate our servant leadership model with an

inverted pyramid that has five sections: Great Purpose, Sacrifice, Raise the Bar, Remove Obstacles, and Celebrate the Individual. We begin at the bottom with Great Purpose because it is the foundation of the pyramid, and it balances all of the values above it.

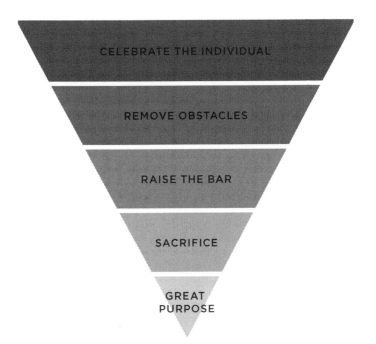

We use the servant leadership model to encourage the practice of striving for excellence, and it reminds our employees that we're on a journey as a team. We do the best we can in all that we do, and after we've raised the bar a notch, we go out and try to exceed the higher standard. This leadership style also helps us in our recognition of teams and individuals in their moments of excellence.

Since this model is so important to me and to my company, I'd like to expand on the significance of each section of the pyramid.

GREAT PURPOSE

Our leaders meet with each team member on a monthly basis for two reasons. The first is to ensure that the employee is meeting the bank's expectations. The second is to make sure that the bank is meeting the *employee's* expectations for personal development and success. Leaders also facilitate a weekly meeting with their team so they don't feel like outsiders in their own organization—leaders share information and ask employees to help them work through problems. These meetings help everyone stay on the same page and to work as a cohesive unit toward the greater purpose of the bank.

SACRIFICE

Our leaders are expected to sacrifice personal ego for the greater good of the organization. They must also give of their time to meet with team members on a regular basis, and they must set aside their need for personal accomplishment to better serve the team. Even though we call this element of the pyramid "sacrifice," we rather view it as leaders *investing* in their team members and in the bank.

RAISE THE BAR

Our leaders set very clear goals for their team members, but they also work with them to stretch and expand upon those goals—they're always thinking of ways to aim even higher. Our organization can't be satisfied with the status quo, so we ask our leaders to actively seek ways to improve our results. Most importantly, leaders hold themselves and their team accountable for performance.

REMOVE OBSTACLES

Our leaders provide constant feedback to team members so they have the best chance at success, but when a team member is not performing well, or it appears that they won't achieve a particular goal, our leaders seek to understand why. What exactly is hindering their success? Once the obstacle is uncovered, the leader and team member work together to remove it and get the employee back on track. If it turns out that an obstacle involves another person or department within the bank, everyone works together to resolve it efficiently while maintaining a positive working relationship and sense of unity.

CELEBRATE THE INDIVIDUAL

Our leaders recognize team members for a job well done, and they do so in a way that is meaningful for the individual and the team. Leaders build close relationships with each team member so they will know how to leverage their gifts and strengths for optimal performance and for the benefit of the organization. Giving employees tasks and responsibilities they will naturally excel in sets everyone up for success!

SERVING OUTSIDE THE COMPANY

To reinforce our company's value of service, we require each employee to volunteer at three nonprofit organizations throughout the year. In addition, they must be in a leadership role at one of them. Some examples of where our employees volunteer include rotary clubs, food banks, or serving as a church elder.

Once an employee makes their choices, they get paid time off to complete their volunteer work, and we further support the organizations through financial contributions. It may seem like we are losing money by paying people to volunteer on company time, but we don't do this for financial gain—it's simply an integral part of our service mission, and our company reaps long-term rewards through this program in the form of employee confidence and loyalty. While we can't measure these mindsets and emotions with data, we do see the results through employee engagement.

THE SERVANT LEADER TOP THREE

There are many people I look up to and strive to emulate in my own way, but there are only three that I consider to be exemplary servant leaders: Mother Teresa, Mahatma Gandhi, and Nelson Mandela, who I've already talked about a bit in Chapter Three.

MOTHER TERESA: A LIFETIME OF HELP

I don't believe that we can talk about serving others without naming my first hero, Mother Teresa. Mother Teresa was a Catholic nun who spent her entire life serving the poorest of the poor in Calcutta, India, and around the world. She helped many people in her lifetime, and my simple words could never describe all that she did. Despite overwhelming odds, she never gave up on her purpose of serving others. She never wanted attention, and she never worried about contracting an illness or disease; she simply treated every person as worthy of her concern and selflessly gave of herself until her final days.

MAHATMA GANDHI: FREEDOM FOR ALL

My second hero, Mahatma Gandhi, dedicated his entire life to helping India gain independence from the British. He was a well-regarded, British-educated lawyer who began practicing law in South Africa. It was during this time that he saw the injustices of the colonial system, and this began his quest to free the people of India from its grasp. He wanted them to live freely with their own indigenous government. Gandhi lived a simple, humble life, and had an unending drive to serve the oppressed. He couldn't have cared less about being the prime minister or a person of influence; he just wanted to help his people. His mission also sparked a great desire in hundreds of nations in Africa, Asia, and the Americas to be freely governed and achieve their own goals, and these countries soon followed his example and began their own movements.

NELSON MANDELA: FAITHFUL SERVANT

I've already discussed the example that my third hero, Nelson Mandela, set regarding the value of faith, but he was also a servant leader—he is more than worthy of being mentioned twice in this book. He was the first president of the independent South Africa, and he easily could have been president for life, but that was of no interest to him. Once he created stability in the nation, he willingly stepped down from his position.

So how does serving others relate to our American Dream? I believe that serving and the American Dream go hand in hand. You'll discover that there are endless rewards when you willingly serve others and help them to learn and grow. Once you do this on a regular basis,

you'll see that giving and serving are much more rewarding than taking and being served!

CHAPTER SEVEN

Humility

—

After I graduated from college, I was ready to quit the night shift at the restaurant. I was eager to do more than wait tables, mop floors, and do dishes, but I had to continue working there until I found a better job. The search seemed endless, and I was frustrated, but continuing to work at the restaurant cultivated true humility in me. I also learned how to lead and manage people under stressful conditions—a skill that would prove helpful to me later on in my career.

Looking back on this experience and many others reinforces my thought that the path to achieving the American Dream is one of humble determination rather than one of aggression and ego. I believe that selling cow dung, mopping floors, and cleaning restrooms created a spirit of humility in me, which has led to my becoming a well-rounded leader who appreciates all work.

DON'T PUT ALL OF YOUR PAST BEHIND YOU

Many people ask why I talk so openly about my upbringing. They believe that since I'm in a position of some leadership, I shouldn't admit to having come from a life of poverty, but I believe the exact opposite. I'm comfortable sharing my background because it made me who I am today. It keeps me humble and grounded, and the life I have now is more wonderful than I ever imagined it would be. I remember walking to school in India and seeing a car pass by and dreaming of having one of my own one day. It seemed like an impossible dream at the time. And now that I can afford a car, I am so grateful to have one!

In the 1970s, I was a young child from a far-off place, and nobody acknowledged me or gave me a second look. The world was very much divided into the haves and have-nots, and if you were a have-not, people didn't give you a chance. Those experiences scarred me emotionally, but they developed my humility, stubborn persistence, and open-minded selflessness. All of those experiences are a part of me, and they made me who I am today, so why should I hide them?

I'M ONLY HUMAN

When I talk to employees and customers, some of them don't know that I'm the bank CEO; if they don't already know my position, I never make it a point to tell them. If they ask what I do at the bank, I say, "Oh, a little bit of everything." I don't want anyone to treat me differently or change their behavior around me because I'm the CEO—I want them to be themselves, and I want them to relate to me as a human being.

A HUMBLE EXAMPLE

I've named many famous people throughout this book who display our American Dream values, but in this chapter, I'd like to talk about a friend who is a poignant example of humility. His spirit and demeanor are warm and welcoming, and he is kind to every person he meets. He is a man of few words, and based on his appearance, you'd probably wonder if he has enough money for lunch, but he has a fifty-year track record of leading successful business ventures. Currently, he has a collection of insurance companies, has significant net worth, and is a prolific philanthropist. However, he never focuses on his wealth, and he never talks about his expertise in business. He's the quintessential everyday guy, and he has a natural way of drawing people to want to be around him.

Building on my friend's inspiration, I want you to remember that humility is built into the fabric of this country, dating back to our founding fathers, like George Washington. If you are a leader, you have a choice: you can be flashy, boisterous, and arrogant, or you can be humble, approachable, and lead in a manner that will positively impact people's lives and will leave a lasting impression on their hearts. Being humble is a quiet strength that inspires people to follow you!

CHAPTER EIGHT

Purpose

The FedEx driver in our area delivers packages to dozens of companies all day long, but he says that our office is his favorite stop. Our employees make him feel welcome, and they energize his day. On the surface, this may not seem like a big deal, but it really is. This is just one of many ways that our company strives to make a positive impact on everyone we meet.

Every leader and every company must look beyond the generation of profits if they truly want to be successful—a greater purpose must drive what they do. When you have a purpose-driven mindset and do good for others, it creates opportunities, has a greater potential impact, and produces rewards for individuals and communities.

My sense of purpose gradually evolved as I transitioned from poverty to living my American Dream. I thought

I would be fulfilled after I graduated from college and became financially comfortable, but I was wrong. I continued to move up in my career, earning higher positions with higher pay, and my children had plenty of food and clothing, but I felt empty inside. Even though I was far away from a life of poverty, I was living an unfulfilled professional life.

I couldn't understand why I felt empty until I realized that I had been counting on goal achievement to bring me happiness rather than a solid purpose. Once I came to this realization, I began to reflect upon what would bring meaning and fulfillment to my life.

If you're a business leader, you are required to focus on the company profits, but you can achieve so much more by helping your employees grow, contributing to your community, and working to make a positive impact on others. If you sincerely follow this path, everything else will fall into place: company growth, the ability to attract talented staff, stature with investors, and money. The path isn't always an easy one, but the rewards of following it are greater than you can imagine, and I experienced great rewards in the past after resigning from a prominent CEO position.

At one point in time, I was the leader of the thirty-fourth largest bank in the country, with a large salary and generous employment agreement. However, the bank didn't believe in or share my values. This was made evident by miserable employees, unhappy customers and investors, and the bank's lack of community involvement. I knew I couldn't be part of an organization that didn't want to positively impact people's lives, and I needed to leave.

I accepted a position at a much smaller bank; I would go from managing 260 branches with 3,400 employees to managing five branches with sixty-two employees. People couldn't believe that I was resigning and that I was going to make less money working for a smaller organization. I was also forfeiting a potentially large cash payout from the pending sale of the bank. Many of them said, "You have to be the dumbest guy we know!" All they could see was that I was leaving a high-ranking position and all that came along with it. If I had an ego, I'm sure I would have stayed, but staying true to my purpose was more important to me than anything else.

I knew in my heart that leaving that organization was the right thing to do. I believe that God saw that my purpose was pure, and he blessed me and the smaller bank for that reason. Within three years, the small bank grew and we sold it. The cash payout I received was four times larger than the one I would have received had I stayed at the large bank! I didn't do what I did for money, but God blessed me with it anyway.

If you take away anything from this story, let it be this: If your purpose is pure, and you aren't driven by ego or greed, it will build upon itself and radiate into spheres of impact and blessing that you never even imagined!

CHICKEN WITH A PURPOSE

Chick-fil-A is a popular fast-food chain restaurant, but they aren't to be compared with McDonald's, Arby's, or Wendy's. Their performance has been consistently phenomenal, with their average store producing two to three times the volume of other fast-food restaurants. This is amazing, considering that they are closed on Sundays!

Chick-fil-A operates with a specific purpose: they want you and your family to have a wonderful experience. They just happen to use chicken as the centerpiece.

This restaurant has never wavered from their purpose of providing the best possible experience *for customers*. From start to finish, they offer special, unexpected touches to their service. They pay attention to every order, and the employees are always kind and friendly. They bring their customers' food to the table and then visit each one, asking if they need refills or anything else.

Indeed, Chick-fil-A has built a reputation on creating a great family dining experience. This is their purpose, and every step they take revolves around it; they've definitely earned their good name and are deserving of their financial success!

DISCOVER YOUR PURPOSE

At the end of the day, our company wants to positively impact people's lives, whether or not they are customers. If we operate with that as our true purpose, I believe that many people eventually *will* become customers because they enjoy being around us and trust what we do. That impact and those relationships are far more long-lasting and valuable than any short-term profits.

When we work with a purpose, it brings joy, contentment, and meaning to everything we do, and it eliminates a great deal of stress from our everyday lives. I found success in my life when I finally focused on a true and pure purpose, and I believe the same will happen for you.

If you have selfish goals, and all you want to do is make a certain amount of money each year, you won't be fulfilled. You'll find long-term success when you work with a true and pure purpose. Take some time to discover what you enjoy and what drives you to get out of bed every day, and your life will be more fulfilling with a clear purpose!

CHAPTER NINE

Boldness

—

As a child, I quickly developed the resolve to never settle for "good enough." My mother inspired us to have audacious goals, and in order to achieve them, we had to do everything we possibly could to have a better life. We sold firewood, stitched more blouses, and studied under the street lights to try and improve our quality of life. We had to be bold and continually take action, knowing that eventually we were going to change our circumstances. In fact, we had to be bold just to survive!

During the long transition from those challenging years to my career today, I believe that mindset of boldness has been one of my greatest assets. For example, early in my career, our company's sales results were lagging, and the entire team felt that our goals were unachievable. I decided to put together a bold strategy and present it to the group. The consensus was that the plan was impossible, but I rallied everyone and said, "Yes, it's possible. Now, let's set a goal and get after it!"

We worked hard, had a lot of fun, and ultimately, we emerged successful. The team discovered that there was great reward in dedicating ourselves to a bold and courageous goal, and in applying ourselves to reach it. After leading this team of people, I developed a reputation for being the go-to guy, and everyone at work knew that I had the drive to get things done. My boldness and commitment in this project helped to jumpstart my career—new opportunities kept coming my way, and senior management began to include me in strategic planning sessions.

A SERIOUS GOAL

I had the incredible chance to put my boldness and drive into action when the board of a small bank in Florida called on me to come and help lead their team. They had $190 million in assets, but they wanted more, so we set a goal for us to reach one billion dollars in three years. The board felt this was an impossible task and that I was just setting unrealistic targets. But they didn't realize that I was absolutely serious and planned to get our entire staff to support that goal.

To make a long story short, we did it! We reached one billion dollars in assets in three years, and we sold the company for a major premium. This goes to show that the combination of humility, focus, and a daring attitude can make great things happen. It's not about being cravenly opportunistic; it's about eschewing the "safe" choice and believing in the possibility of more. Have the courage to be bold!

APPLY YOUR POTENTIAL WITH BOLDNESS

I see a great deal of highly creative, intelligent twenty- and thirty-somethings who have much potential, but they won't veer from a certain path—they don't want to rock the boat or take the calculated risk. My hope is that they will develop a new, bolder mindset; otherwise, ten to fifteen years from now, they might feel that their lives are full of what-ifs. They will have regrets because they didn't have the courage to step out and do something they are passionate about.

Taking the safe route wastes your God-given talents, and it certainly won't bring you fulfillment in life. Don't let opportunities pass you by because you are afraid of rejection or because you doubt your abilities; take steps of faith and take some risks. You have to stretch in order to grow and discover all of the amazing things you are capable of! Even when your desired end result seems far out of reach, you need to keep your eyes on it, or you will never get there.

I encourage you to begin working toward your dreams, but when you do, please be wise and discerning. It's important to draw a line between boldness and recklessness. Don't take action every time a new idea runs through your head, and don't pursue a different path until you've had a chance to think it through. I also suggest that you run your plans and ideas by people who have your best interests at heart so they can help you make the best possible decisions.

STEPPING OUT IN BOLDNESS

If you are still hesitant to pursue your dreams, this next story might change your mind.

A bank that I worked for early in my career began delegating projects and giving new assignments to employees. This was in addition to their regular workload, and many of them viewed these assignments as burdens rather than opportunities.

One morning, the bank CEO approached me and said, "Andrew, we're gathering some leaders together, and I'd like for you to talk with them about pursuing these new opportunities with passion." Of course, I readily agreed. I had experienced some success in my career, and my company openly recognized me as a problem solver and go-getter, but I wanted more. I had aspirations of becoming a CEO—I wanted to lead and inspire teams.

Giving this talk was a chance for me to put myself on the map, but I also looked forward to sharing a positive message that would hopefully spark new courses of action within the company. In short, I spoke to the group about recognizing everything as an opportunity rather than as a challenge or distraction. I encouraged them to look for ways to do bigger and better things in the future.

After the talk, I asked our CEO how he knew that he wanted to be a CEO and how he attained the position. He walked me through his career path, and he shared the common traits of successful leaders. I thought I possessed these traits, so when he was finished, I put myself out there and told him that I wanted to be a CEO too. He fully understood and supported my goal, but he said that my chances were slim since the company only filled C-suite positions with people who lived near the headquarters and I lived too far away. If I was serious about becoming CEO, I'd have to relocate my family.

I liked my position at the company—the salary was good, and I was comfortable, but I knew that if I wasn't working toward becoming a CEO, I wasn't realizing my full potential. After the bank CEO set realistic expectations for me, I didn't stick with the company and accept the limitation. Instead of relocating, I took a risk and found a job with another bank in the area—one that had a potential path toward becoming CEO. This bold step paid off for me, as it became the first CEO opportunity of many in my career.

JERRY JONES'S BOLD MOVE

When I think of boldness, I think of the current owner of the Dallas Cowboys, Jerry Jones.

Jones, a lifelong football fan, was an offensive lineman for the University of Arkansas in the early 1960s and dreamed of owning an NFL team someday. He got his chance when the Dallas Cowboys were up for sale in the late 1980s. Despite having a successful business background, he didn't have enough money to acquire the team, but Jones didn't let that stop him. Leveraging everything he had and borrowing whatever he could, Jones gathered enough money to make his dream a reality, and he's been owner of the Dallas Cowboys since 1989.

But Jones didn't stop there—he continued to display his bold character in his new role. The Cowboys were struggling when he first bought the team, with his first ownership season ending with a record of 1-15. Jones decided to fire longtime head coach Tom Landry, a decision that was both drastic and unpopular. However, within a few years, the Cowboys were winning Super Bowls, and the franchise is now worth about $4.5 billion.

Jones could have played it safe, but he was bold and put everything on the line. He grabbed his dream with passion, and as a result, he's creating a lasting legacy for his children, grandchildren, and of course, Dallas Cowboy fans.

To create new opportunities, you have to make bold decisions and go after your passion. Step out in faith, and pursue your dreams!

CHAPTER TEN

Legacy

———

I don't believe that we are here to work until we retire and then spend our remaining days in leisure—we are here to make a mark in this world. When all is said and done and we prepare to depart from this earth, wouldn't it be wonderful to know that we are leaving a lasting legacy?

In this life, we have the incredible opportunity to display kindness, honesty, and integrity to others and encourage them to follow our example. What we give, do, and say to our spouse, children, friends, and coworkers all work together to build a legacy. As a family man and a leader in the banking industry, it's of the utmost importance to me to display excellence in all that I do, knowing that my children, grandchildren, and employees are watching me. I want them to see and remember a positive example.

I'm establishing a new bank at the moment, and almost

every leader in the group is under the age of forty. This was an intentional arrangement because our ultimate goal is to inspire and spread the concept of building a company with a great purpose. We want to create a hunger in the growing leaders of today, show them that success entails much more than making money, and in turn, we hope that they will pass this along to the next generation of leaders.

THE LEGACY OF GEORGE H.W. BUSH

I can think of no better example of someone leaving an impactful legacy than the late former president, George H.W. Bush. It was incredible and fascinating to see how Republicans and Democrats alike came together for a few days to honor him after his passing.

It might be a little-known fact that Bush never aspired to be president—his main focus was to care for his family and to be a good and decent person. However, people recognized him as a man of integrity; no one ever had a bad thing to say about him, and his character eventually led him to become the leader of our nation. He's known for coining the phrase, "a thousand points of light" in reference to volunteerism, and what he said in his January 20, 1989, inaugural address still holds true today:

I have spoken of a thousand points of light, of all the community organizations that are spread like stars throughout the Nation, doing good. We will work hand in hand, encouraging, sometimes leading, sometimes being led, rewarding. We will work on this in the White House, in the Cabinet agencies. I will go to the people and the programs that are the brighter points of light, and I will ask every member of my government to become involved. The old ideas are new again because they are not old, they are timeless: duty, sacrifice, commitment, and a patriotism that finds its expression in taking part and pitching in.

Although he was in a position of power, Bush continued to serve others with generosity and a kind and gracious spirit, and he imbued a sense of trust in everyone with whom he interacted. He proved that legacy is not in a name, or in having a building named after you—it's not in any tangible thing. Legacy is what you leave behind *within* people. With one son following in his footsteps to become president of the United States and another the governor of Florida, it's safe to say that he left behind a proud and lasting legacy.

ALL IN THE FAMILY

Another perfect example of establishing a legacy comes from a family I once had the privilege to work with. In 1998, I helped a hardworking mother and her two children secure a small loan to open a hardware store. They opened the store with the intent of providing hardware products and services, but they also wanted to serve the community. Today, they are an extremely successful local business, with five stores and over 150 employees!

Recently, the woman's son called to thank me for helping them with their first loan. "Your help made a tremendous difference in our lives. Now here we are, thirty years later, with five stores and forty-three family members in the business. We wanted to thank you and your staff for helping us get started."

The longevity and growth of this family's hardware store is impressive, especially when they've had to compete against large corporations like Home Depot and Lowe's. I believe they found success because they never lost sight of their purpose. They realized their dream of opening a store and focusing on serving the needs of their community. They've built an incredible family and community legacy in the process.

YOUR PERSONAL LEGACY

I firmly believe that you and I can do the same thing. It's difficult to focus on legacy-minded actions today, but I want you to remember that life goes by very quickly. Make the best of every single moment and behave in ways that leave people feeling that you're honest, straightforward, and gracious. Always say what you mean, and mean what you say. Living intentionally is like building a war chest of positive attributes that becomes your legacy. I guarantee that you'll be more successful in business and in your personal life by doing so, even in the midst of conflict.

Don't let fear or your ego get in the way and wait for others to take the initiative in certain matters; be the first one to ask for forgiveness or to start a new conversation. I'm never afraid to apologize when I know that I'm wrong or if I've raised my voice. It may seem like an act of weakness to apologize, but it will make your relationships stronger, and you will create a lasting legacy of kindness and humility.

Conclusion

———

At the beginning of my life, I was a poor, skinny kid collecting cow dung in India, sleeping on a cow dung floor, and scrambling for food. I've come a long way since those days, and I'm near the end of an invigorating career, but I've never forgotten my humble beginnings. My personal experience of leaving poverty to become a husband, proud father, and business leader in the United States should be evidence that the American Dream is alive and well. It's real, and I believe that anyone can attain it.

My hope is that you have been inspired by this book and that the values I've shared drive you to follow your dreams. Ignore the naysayers and have faith! If you believe in yourself and remember all that we've discussed in these pages, every dream will be within your reach. I urge you to remember and practice the following values and principles:

- **Focus:** Dedicate attention and energy to particular tasks and eliminate distractions. Be disciplined and intentional in cultivating your focus!
- **Persistence:** Develop long-term attention to the areas of focus in your life. It won't happen overnight; you have to keep at it.
- **Faith:** Trust and believe in a higher power, and don't just pray for the present—pray for the future also.
- **Authenticity:** Be real, honest, and even vulnerable with others. Don't be afraid to show your true self.
- **Family:** Embrace the love, support, and stability of family, and work to create a cohesive family unit. This applies to immediate and extended family.
- **Service:** Serving others is an essential part of success. Become a servant leader.
- **Humility:** All that you have and all that you accomplish is a gift. Don't let pride take over your motivations.
- **Purpose:** We all have a calling and a compelling reason for doing what we do. Once you discover your purpose, stay true to it!
- **Boldness:** Be audacious in your goals and take steps to achieve them, no matter how daring you need to be.
- **Legacy:** Your life and work can reach beyond just what you do today. Think of the lasting impact of your words and actions, and remember that everything has the potential to become your legacy.

The American dream is achievable, but I can say with absolute certainty that following someone else's path to success will lead to a dead end. Set high expectations for yourself, and don't try to be who someone else expects you to be. Believe in your purpose, hold on to it, and you will emerge all the better.

At this moment, I want you to cast aside all doubts, old and new, and begin to pursue your dreams with a clear focus. Regardless of your background, race, or upbringing, you can be anything if you work hard and apply yourself, and cultivate the life you've always dreamed of. This is *Our American Dream*!

Now, go out there and make it happen!

About the Author

—

ANDREW SAMUEL, who serves as the Chairman, CEO, and Director of LINKBANCORP, Inc. and LINK-BANK, has a long track record of industry success. He's helped take banks from insignificance to being listed on the Nasdaq Global Market and has been involved in the mergers and acquisitions of more than ten companies with an aggregate deal value surpassing $1.5 billion. Andrew has shaped workplaces that are listed as the best to work at in their region and has created cultures centered around servant leadership. Andrew lives in the central Pennsylvania area with his wife of thirty-six years. They're blessed with five daughters, four sons-in-law, and twelve grandchildren.

Made in the USA
Columbia, SC
22 December 2019